Wendell Johnson, Professor of Speech Pathology and Psychology, University of Iowa and editor of Speech Handicapped School Children, writes that self-expression, self-communication, and communication between the speaker and other persons are the fundamental purposes of speech. According to Professor Johnson,

{ a speech disorder occurs when all of the basic functions of speech are affected to some degree and, in certain cases, one function may be more seriously disturbed than another (6).

My little bradda not mento, so you betta stop teasing him all da time jus cuz you tink you can talk more betta dan him. Jus cuz you can go one regula-kine school—not da special-kine school whea da teacha clamp one rula-looking kine ting on your tongue.

Wot? You no believe me?

I saw yum fo real kine. I promise! I dunno why da teacha did dat to him. Jus cuz my litto bradda get hard time fo talk no mean he stupid. He no can—was dat word again—arteekcolate? My fadda tease him all da time. Call him "short tongue". Sometimes Popo Lum, da landlady downstairs, talk to Harold-Boy like he deaf and dumb or someting.

Sheeze.

He only four years old, try.

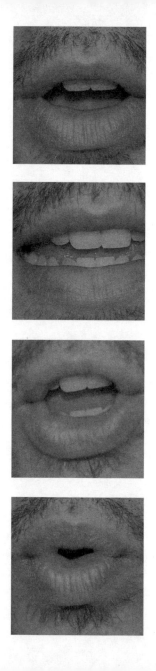

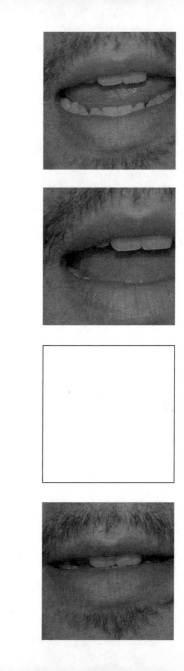

Articulation: when tongue, jaw, teeth, lips, and palate alter the air stream coming from the vocal cords creating sounds, which make up syllables, which make up words. The most important structure of articulation is the tongue, which is responsible for effecting the changes in the mouth basic to the production of all but a few sounds. The tongue is so essential to human speech, languages are often referred to as "tongues" (Hanson 1-9).

I hold my madda's hand everytime da school bus from da special school come fo take Harold-Boy away. Insai dat bus get funny-kine looking childrens. E, I bet dey hate for talk too. One boy look like he stay wearing one bird cage ova his head. Only his eyes move. Get one girl wit magnifying glasses—da kine for kill ants—strap to her head. She get metal sticks stuck to her legs too. Get one nodda girl who no can stay still. She use to pull out her hair beefo da bus driva wen force her for wear white seat belts across her chest and her legs. And get one supa skinny boy, he just stare at my bradda.

'Wot you looking at?" I yell.

"Badda you?"

Da skinny boy no say nutting. Gala gala drips from his crooked lip. His collar stay all wet.
"Be good now," I tell my little bradda. "Bum-bye wen you come home we go watch cartoon, kay?"

The body of the tongue is shaped like a broad-based anvil; the body is what we see when we look into the mouth. The body of the tongue is divided into four parts: the tip, the blade, the front, and the back. What we cannot see when we look into the mouth is the tongue's root. (Hanson 1-9)

Creole languages are primarily born out of necessity. In his 1936 article, "The Competition of Languages in Hawaii," Dr. John E. Reinecke, whose scholarly work has contributed to the scientific study of Creole languages, defines a Creole dialect by describing its function in plantation communities:

> **A Creole dialect is a greatly simplified, makeshift form of a European language which has arisen in master-servant situations on a large scale between European employers and (usually) non-European laborers. It is especially common in plantation regions, and is necessary where the laborers are drawn from several linguistic groups.**

(7)

Reinecke points out that the formation of a Creole language met the need for a "medium of communication between members of non-English speaking groups" (Reinecke 105).

In many cases, plantation labor populations were so ethnically diverse that a Creole language became the only feasible means of communication between the different ethnic groups–

–a common tongue of the working class.

This lingua franca was not only used between groups of multi-ethnic laborers, it was also used between the laborers and the plantation "masters." Reinecke writes that it would be impossible for the plantation "master" to become proficient in every language of the ethnically diverse labor groups; therefore Creole was also used as a "language of command" (18) because "masters rarely deign to learn the speech of the servile population" (18).

Plantation "masters" used Creole languages to create class stratification between "master" and "servant" laborer. Creole languages were also used to enforce and maintain that class stratification by keeping the laborer ignorant of the "master's" ruling class language. Joseph Vendryes, author of Language: A Linguistic Introduction to History, writes Creoles were once considered the speech of " inferior beings... a subordinate class whose superiors have never troubled nor desired to make them speak any language correctly " (Vendryes qtd. in Reinecke 18).

At firs my madda was supa worried dat Harold-Boy neva start talking da same time as me and my cousin dem. Now she stay mo worried, because he no can talk like everybody else. But, not like everybody in dis house talk good English. My madda, she every time tell me,

"you not going get one good job if you no can talk good English. People going tink you stupid."

Stupid?

Gee, no wonda she stay all
hu-hu about Harold-Boy.
Me, at leese I can talk. But
Harold-Boy… das one
different story. He get
one—watchoo call—one
speech impedment. Das why
dey treat him like he mento.
Piss me off.

My litto bradda no belong on dat bus wit all dose handicap freaks.

There is a general understanding among listeners of a language that identifies whether a sound comes within what is considered normal limits or whether we sense something is wrong or misarticulated. This impression of misarticulation may be generally referred to as baby talk, lazy tongue movement, or any other variety of descriptive terms that imply the listener has some trouble understanding what is being said (Rousey 34).

Only me can undahstand wot Harold-Boy trying fo say.

Itah, itah: sister.

Wuh-yol: world.

Too-too, too-too: Popeye da Sailor Man.

Harold-Boy smile up wen Popeye squeeze da
can, eat da spinach, beat up Brutus. Harold-Boy,
he make oojee kine face wen Olive Oil like kiss
Popeye all ova, and he love to sing along wit da
Popeye song.

You like **undahstand** my bradda or wot?

Try let him sing.

What kind of social implications does a "language of command" created for "master-servant" environments have upon the descendants of that "servile population," especially when those descendants continue to use an evolved form of that Creole generations later–after the plantation has closed down, and the laborer is revered as an ancestor? Today, half of the State of Hawai'i's population of approximately one million people speaks Hawai'i Creole English (HCE) (Romaine 527).

I am one voice out of that one million.

I was born and raised in Honolulu, Hawai'i. My father is of Hawaiian, Chinese ancestry, and my mother, Filipino, Japanese. My genealogy can be traced back to Japanese pig farmers in Happy Valley, Maui; Chinese and Filipino immigrant plantation workers; and Native Hawaiians from the island of Hawai'i; however, I am not fluent in any of my ancestors' native tongues. **Instead I speak** both Standard English and Hawai'i Creole English, or "Pidgin," which is what the language has been called since its inception.

Local Hawai'i people are raised to believe that Pidgin is reserved for less formal social environments, i.e. **family gatherings or lunch hour conversation**, and should never be spoken in "formal" professional and academic settings. Pidgin also functions as **"an identifier of in-group and out-group populations"** (Yamamoto 21). In other words, Pidgin is a social marker indicating who is and is not local. Whenever we choose to speak Pidgin, **we are conscious of Pidgin's power to include and exclude.** Go bus out da Pidgin wen trying fo get one kama'aina discount from da local guy or gal behind da rent-a-car counta. Garrans da haole tourist at da same counta going pay mo money fo rent one car.

Despite its widespread use as a marker of local identity, HCE also carries negative connotations. The late Charlene Sato, who was once the chair of the University of Hawai'i TESOL program, described the social contradictions that HCE speakers face.

It is undeniable that negative stereotypes of HCE and positive stereotypes of SE (Standard English) are still held by many in the community. Even as a marker of working class and ethnic (actually, non-Caucasian) identity in the past, HCE was arguably perceived as more of a stigma than an asset.

(656-7)

Although this attitude towards HCE has changed in recent years via vibrant performance art, literature, and music of Hawai'i, **residuals of that stigma still exist.** John Mirikitani, a one time Board of Education candidate, expressed his opinion of Hawai'i Creole English in Michael Tsai's 1995 Honolulu Weekly article, "Pondering Pidgin."

It seems to me that Pidgin hasn't developed the level of sophistication [that standard English has]. English-language mastery correlates with getting jobs in Western society. Studies show that billions of dollars are lost because people can't get jobs due to illiteracy. It seems that if you can speak English, you can improve the economy.

(4)

This stigma has made it necessary for Pidgin speakers to learn how to code shift from HCE into Standard English for more formal situations (i.e. job interviews, board rooms, research papers). This learned "necessity" tacitly perpetuates the assumed superiority of Standard English over Hawai'i Creole English, which in turn reinforces the assumption that speakers of Pidgin are intellectually and socially inferior to speakers of Standard English, or as Mirikitani would assume, unsophisticated, illiterate, and unemployed.

Studies done on sociolinguistic attitudes in Hawai'i indicate that "HCE is associated with low academic achievement and low socioeconomic status" (Sato 652). One such study completed by Jody Yamamoto at the University of Hawai'i indicated that HCE speakers are generally perceived to be intellectually inferior:

> Speech varieties in Hawai'i are perceptible and over all stereo typing does exist consistently for speakers of all varieties . . **Standard speakers are Caucasian and of high educational/occupational status** while nonstandard speakers are non-Caucasian and of lower educational/status.
>
> (84)

Local Hawai'i students and teachers participated in these studies. Such is the paradox of local pride and self-loathing that is characteristic of Hawai'i Creole English speakers. Pidgin is not only the emblem of the Hawai'i plantation era; it has also been perceived as a stigma indicating low social status, ignorance, and local identity.

The tongue is comprised of multidirectional muscle fibers which are divided into two groups: intrinsic, which originate and end within the tongue, and extrinsic, which have one attachment outside the tongue (Hanson 12-13).

About a decade after Captain James Cook "discovered" the Hawaiian Islands in 1778, Pacific fur trade vessels began voyaging between America and the commercial ports of China, making brief stops in Hawai'i's harbors (Carr 3). Throughout the late 1700s and early 1800s, traders and merchants of an ever increasing sandalwood trade began to bargain in a reduced form of English. By the 1820s, the whaling industry had replaced the sandalwood trade, and a "pidgin" English could be heard in port communities from Honolulu to Lahaina to Hilo. The blending of Hawaiian, English, and Cantonese created many of the Pidgin words we use today.

Intrinsic muscles change the tongue's shape: curling the tip of the tongue back, narrowing and widening the blade, or flattening and rounding the front (Hanson 12-3).

The 1820s also marked the arrival of the American missionaries who realized that **the only way to convert Native Hawaiians** to Christianity was to learn the Hawaiian language. With a zealous conviction, American missionaries **reduced and altered** what was once exclusively an oral language to a written one. They translated and then printed the Bible, mission schools were established on all of the islands, and "religious instruction formed the basis for formal education in Hawai'i" (Kawamoto 196).

By 1824, Queen Regent Ka'ahumanu's conversion to Christianity sparked the Kingdom's first education law, which declared her support for missionary-led education, and many native leaders ruled under the influence of Western 'advisers' (Kawamoto 196). However, Western influence was not limited to language and education. Foreigners brought with them **disease that devastated the Native Hawaiian population**, and "this decline deepened the feeling of hopeless discouragement in the face of Western culture… Economic and administrative necessities combined to give English currency and prestige at the expense of the native language… The Hawaiian with a knowledge of English could often obtain a position with a haole firm" (Reinecke 32). By the 1870s, English inevitably became the administrative language of the Hawaiian Islands.

The extrinsic muscles work with the intrinsic muscles to alter tongue position within the oral cavity. What is most pertinent to the tongue's movement, function, and power is that no single muscle works alone (Hanson 12-13).

In 1835, a young Boston businessman named William Hooper established the first sugar plantation in Koloa, Kaua'i (Kawamoto 196), which marked the beginning of a plantation industry that would spread throughout Hawai'i. The plantations were primarily worked by Native Hawaiians, but in order to meet the needs of a rapidly growing labor-intensive industry, plantation owners imported immigrant laborers: the Chinese in 1852, the Japanese beginning in 1868, and the Filipinos in 1907 (Tsai 4).

Political incorporation into the U.S. began with the overthrow of the Native Hawaiian monarchy in 1893, which was followed by annexation to the U.S. in 1899. By 1896, English was declared the required language of instruction in all schools. Elitist American business and religious establishments had two motives for teaching the English language: religious conversion and the American colonization of Hawai'i's indigenous people (Kawamoto 200).

Plantation owners were not about to enforce a policy to "Americanize" immigrant children via English language proficiency and education, because "the spread of education, haole attitudes and skills made traditional plantation life less and less attractive… It seemed as if the ideals of Americanization and mass education were in direct contradiction with the needs of the sugar industry" (Shi qtd in Kawamoto 199).

Conditions which precipitate and maintain articulation defects after the child has begun to speak are only an extension of the conditions which limited the production and differentiation of sounds and which interfered with the development of a communication attitude before he began to speak (Curtis 65).

The contract laborer was usually ignorant not only of the native language but of English as well; he was in a dependent position because of his lack of money, his legal bonds, and his ignorance of conditions; he was tied for some years to a plantation in a rural district which undeveloped transportation often made remote from the capital… and he was exposed to very limited social and linguistic contacts with his bosses and the native population.

(Reinecke 40)

Because a contract laborer socialized usually with other members of his or her own ethnic community, exposure to Standard English was limited to work under the "lunas." These plantation "bosses" gave instructions in a condensed, minimal form of English mixed with Cantonese pidgin- "can do," "no can," "bumbye," etc. The laborers began to imitate the lunas, and developed their own form of a pidginized English later to be deemed Hawai'i Pidgin English (HPE) (Carr 6). But HPE took on a different function; as Charlene Sato explains, it served "as a secondary mode of communication for speakers who conducted the bulk of their interactions in their native tongue" (259).

Despite the segregation policies of plantation owners, HPE and later HCE served as the means by which different immigrant groups could form a single identity. This was especially important to the plantation laborers' children who could neither connect ancestrally with their own native culture nor to a relatively foreign mainstream American culture. "By being 'local', one could maintain a sense of ethnic identity while at the same time identifying with a larger, more encompassing culture" (Kawamoto 201).

Hawai'i became a territory of the United States in 1900, and the majority of children born in Hawai'i were theoretically U.S. citizens. Compulsory education policies required that the children of plantation workers attend public school. By this time Hawai'i's economic and political affiliations with the United States had grown, along with an ever increasing English-speaking population, which was comprised of "middle-level plantation management… physicians, teachers, social workers, …and members of the military," (Hughes 85) who were able to send their children to the limited number of English-language private schools. Consequently, plantation children were separated from their native English-speaking peers through the English Standard School System which was implemented in 1924.

All too often any attempt to single out . . . the 'behavior problem' children or the speech handicapped, in order to give them the care and training they need, has resulted in their being stigmatized or 'socially branded' as different in some unsavory sense.

. . . we can sometimes do as much harm by applying derogatory labels to children as we can by outright physical attempts to maim them (Johnson 51).

The English Standard School System was the result of a 1920 study of schools in Hawai'i completed by the U.S. Bureau of Education. The Bureau's final report was to reveal any institutionalized race and class inequalities toward non-native speakers of English in the public schools, but in actuality, the report justified segregation.

Many white people, Hawaiians, and Part-Hawaiians, who can afford to pay tuition, but who would like perhaps for democratic impulses to send their children to the public high schools, are deterred from doing so... their children would be outnumbered in their classes by the Orientals, who have little in common with them and whose language difficulties impede the progress of all.

(qtd in Hughes 69)

The bureau's study recommended that entrance into the English Standard School System require that a child pass an oral exam, and if appropriate, a written English language test. If students could be admitted on the basis of English language proficiency, then ancestry and class discrimination could be furtively incorporated into the education system under the apparent motive of promoting 'good' English. "In fact, it [the study] was an effort to remove these [Caucasian] children from the 'corrupting influences' of the non-Caucasian youngsters" (Kawamoto 202).

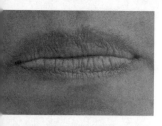

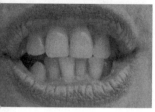

Whenever we deal with a speech disorder, disturbance or problem, there is a peculiarly general and fundamental notion to be introduced. It is this: a problem has members. The speaker is not the only member of an articulation or voice problem. In certain cases possibly all of the speaker's listeners are also members of the problem. Some members are more important than others. In working with any speech, voice, language, or hearing problem-any communication problem-it is essential that you find out who the main members of the problem are (Johnson 6).

In her 1993 article, "The Demise of the English Standard School System," Judith R. Hughes writes that those in favor of the 1924 English Standard School System claimed that the immigrant children of plantation workers were a "direct threat" to the American children's educational advancement:

> **(1) children from English-speaking homes were held back by the large numbers of children who had trouble with the language; (2) in almost all schools there were not enough American-ancestry children so that they could exercise the... 'Americanizing' that supporters of integrated classes wanted; and (3) English-speaking parents, who were taxpayers, had a right to an appropriate public education.**

(70)

The English Standard School System was obviously a ploy to segregate children by race and class under the guise of "educational concerns." The plan "worked against integration of the non-English speaking children into the community in which they lived and in which they would become voters" (Hughes 70). Ironically, one of the results of isolating Creole speaking children was that they communicated with each other exclusively through the use of HPE. Everyday conversations at home with family members were instrumental in HPE's evolution into the more structured and stabilized Hawai'i Creole English.

Between the late 1930s and the early 1940s, second and third generation children of immigrant families began speaking Creole exclusively (Kawamoto 200). But as a result of the English Standard School System, an ever-increasing military presence and a growing tourism trade, Pidgin was perceived as an impairment to one's education, entering the job market, and Hawai'i's future in general. In a handbook for elementary teachers titled Hawaii's Speech Needs: Analysis and Improvement of Island Speech, written and published by the Department of Public Instruction, Territory of Hawai'i, 1949, teachers were informed that Hawai'i children were severely at a a disadvantage because of the way they spoke:

The dialectal speech problems of Hawai'i are often so serious as to constitute real stumbling blocks to success. Islanders are handicapped in maintaining happy, successful, professional and social relationships because of their poor English... We cannot overlook the fact that many people are clinging to pidgin as their chief language and are growing up with serious handicaps to vocational success... some teachers become over anxious, undermine the wholesome development of children in their overzealous attempts to improve speech.

(1)

Stigmatized by its planta-
tion origins, many felt that
Hawai'i Creole English was
a cultural legacy that was
better left for dead
(Romaine 101). This atti-
tude surfaced in academic
publications and public
newspapers throughout the
State of Hawai'i.

Some Light on the Problem of Bilingualism

As Found from a Study of the Progress

in Mastery of English Among Pre-

school Children of Non-American

Ancestry in Hawaii

Madorah E. Smith

1939

Teachers College, University of Hawaii

I. INTRODUCTION

A. The Problem

The purpose of this investigation is threefold. First, it is a survey of the comparative progress made in the mastery of the English language on the part of the young children of different racial antecedents in the Territory of Hawaii, so that we many know better what to expect of the children of different racial groups at the time of school entrance and the Americanization of each group, so far as that they may be measured by the use of its national language.

Second, it is an attempt to study a number of factors that may hinder or further the children in such mastery.

Third, since the languages spoken in Hawaii are many, and many of the children are bilingual, it is an attempt to throw a little light on the problem of whether or not bilingualism is a hindrance in the mastery of speech to very young children (123).

IS THE HANDICAP DUE ONLY TO PIDGIN ENGLISH
OR ALSO TO BILINGUALISM?

...it is apparent that the non-haole children in Hawaii are retarded in language development. Not a single racial group studied has attained at six years the use of sentences as long on the average as those that the five-year-old Caucasian monoglots use. When they speak English, the number of errors per thousand words averages for every group higher than the number which the monoglots make at three years of age.

ANALYSIS OF CONVERSATIONS BY PARTS OF SPEECH

Inflection of Words

Considering the use of verbal forms, we find the Island Children to be much retarded... In general in the use of the different parts of speech and of inflected forms of the words, the Island children are retarded. (210)

V. SUMMARY AND CONCLUSIONS

A. Summary

7. The results show that in comparison with haole children and those studied on the mainland, the Island children are seriously retarded in the use of the English language, a retardation which is not compensated for by a greater advancement in other languages used. (266)

B. Conclusions

The children in Hawaii from non-haole homes are retarded in language development to a degree so marked that, on most criteria, at the time of school entrance they are at about the level of three-year old children from a less polyglot environment. The retardation is due to two handicaps: the prevalent use of pidgin English, and the bilingualism of many homes. (271)

In the article, "A Study of the Causes of Feelings of Inferiority" published in The Journal of Psychology in 1938, Madorah E. Smith examined the numerous reasons for experiencing "conflict over difference," better known in layman's terms as an "inferiority complex." She explains, "The term 'conflict over difference' was used rather than the more familiar 'inferiority complex' in order to emphasize the fact that it includes what is usually considered to be a mark of superiority" (Smith 315).

Smith asked students to anonymously list their experiences with the different conflicts. A total of 219 students had contributed 700 conflicts ranging from feeling inferior about one's "shape of face" to one's "ignorance of American customs." The "conflicts" also listed were "poor English," and "speaking mother-tongue poorly." Smith's study reveals that her subjects felt inferior because they had not mastered their mother-tongue and English.

The difference between 'speaking mother-tongue poorly' and 'speaking English poorly' is a significant one, it being 3.8 times its standard error. In every group except the haoles, ...the proportion checking 'poor English' is less than that checking 'speaking mother-tongue poorly.' Yet English is the language of the Islands and of the public schools and the school teachers will tell you that the English usage of the majority of the non-haole children in Hawai'i is very faulty. Either their knowledge of their mother-tongue is even worse or they more frequently are made to feel their lack in that respect.

(322)

Smith goes on to write about the response of a Chinese student who was asked a question in her native Chinese language. When the student's sister answered the question, she was ridiculed for her "faulty" use of Chinese. Smith's conclusion: "Perhaps the student's inferiority in English is felt only when at school and that in the mother tongue at all other times" (Smith 322).

Only me can undahstand wot
Harold-Boy trying fo say.

What is tragic about these findings is that **Pidgin was the result of a multi-ethnic working class's attempt at <u>solidarity</u>.**

Cultural elitism reduced that attempt to a handicap. The education policies of the time were schizophrenic in nature. First, Standard English was imposed on children of immigrant parents, then the children were separated from native-English speakers, then the children were labeled "inferior" and "ignorant" (Hughes 70) because they could not speak Standard English. In addition to feeling inferior about their second language skills, these students also felt inadequate in regard to speaking their own mother tongues.

I bet they hate fo talk too.

Hughes explains why the English Standard School System was finally abolished after the 1950s–after World War II:

After World War II the Democratic party in Hawai'i became the bastion of reform-minded Asian-Americans, **...who had not been represented in the English standard system. One of the main planks of the newly empowered Democratic Party was the ending of the dual schools. This was tied to some extent to the drive for statehood. They feared that people on the mainland would con-clude that the territory was not ready for statehood if it had to maintain special schools for people who spoke Standard English.**

(85)

Political and economic ties with the United States had increased, and the working class migrated from plantation to urban areas. Tourism had replaced sugar as the primary economic resource, and contact with standard-English-speaking tourists from the Mainland increased.

When Hawai'i became a state in 1959, Standard English speakers were perceived as more sophisticated and intelligent than Pidgin speakers. An example of this perception was a Honolulu journalist's opinion in the editorial pages of the *Honolulu Star Bulletin* on December 13, 1947:

> **There is no excuse for pidgin spoken by native Hawaiians who had the advantages of American education. Perhaps I have a mania on the subject, but I am convinced that unless a person can speak well, he cannot think well. Substituting the expression, "da kine" for every word lacking in one's vocabulary is not only an indication of verbal poverty, but of limited capacity for thought as well.**

(24)

Itah, itah - Sister.

I gave Hal his baby shower gift.

"All right!," he yelled. "Harold and The Purple Crayon. Classic. Tanks Sis."

Hal flashed a shaka sign to me from across the living room crowded with future in-laws and friends. I returned the gesture. He remembered, I say to myself. Does he remember the way he held the first edition of that book close to his chest as he walked up to the librarian's counter some thirty years ago?

When Hal was little he loved to see his name printed on the cover of that book; he borrowed it over and over. The Harold in the book is a boy that wears footed pajamas while he walks through the pages creating rooms and escape routes with a single purple crayon and the page's white space. When Hal was a little boy he looked a lot like the purple crayon Harold. Both were small-framed, not particularly frail looking, but heedful in expression.

Whenever my parents referred to Hal's speech problems, they used the phrase "short tongue," which created the image of a pink stub squirming to get out of his mouth. Hal's tongue wasn't literally short. He was a "late talker," and couldn't articulate certain words or speak in complete sentences until long after the "normal" expected age. Way before research was done on late-talking children, they had been conveniently labeled as "retarded," or diagnosed with "pervasive developmental disorder" or "autism." These labels were a major source of distress for my parents and caused all sorts of problems for my brother.

But that was a long time ago.

Speech characteristics once created, tend to
affect the personality in ways that insure their
further development. Having begun to speak
hesitantly, even a little hesitantly, the child runs
the risk of meeting with reactions from others
that make it likely that he will speak more
hesitantly next time (Johnson 75).

"So wot you going name da baby?" I asked Hal.

He looked at his fiancée.

"We like the name Kai," she answered.

"Kai Kanae?" I said. "Eh brah, you one poet and you don't know it."

"Nah brah," Hal said, "You da poet. You da one wit da brains."

I looked down at my hands. "Not." I said.

"Grad school right?" Hal asked me.

"So."

"So?"

"Yeah. So?" I asked.

"I couldn't go to graduate school." Hal said.

"Das not true. You could do it." I said. "Pass me da camera. Let me get a picture of you wit all dese presents."

Hal handed the camera to his future mother-in-law, who passed it to his future brother-in-law, who then passed it to his future father-in-law, who passed the camera to me. I focused in on Hal's face through the camera's viewfinder. Inside the black framed tunnel, I saw a quiet young man who is the elegant mixture of Hawaiian, Chinese, Filipino, and Japanese. I wondered if his new in-laws understood why he was so shy, so painfully introverted.

You like undahstand him or wot?

"Say, shi-shi diaper!" I yelled as I lined up the shot.

Hal covered his face with a case of disposable diapers right before I snapped the picture. He laughed, and then kissed his fiancée on her forehead, a rare display of public affection from a man who preferred to be invisible when he was a little boy.

When he was little, a few of Hal's favorite hiding places were under the clothes racks at Sears & Roebucks, up in the lichee tree, behind the water heater, and under the stairs that led to our front door. Hal, who had to see a speech therapist when he was four years old, would hide under those stairs when the Easter Seals School bus pulled up into our driveway. Most of the other children in the bus suffered from some sort of developmental disorder. They grunted, sniffled, or cried. Other children simply stared back at us blank and indifferent. In order to get Hal on the bus, Mom and I would bribe him with a Popeye Pez dispenser. Hal would climb up into the bus, find his way to a window seat, and wave a miniature Popeye head at us while he sang too-too, too-too–the sound Popeye's pipe makes at the end of the cartoon's jingle.

"Who like cake?" my mother yelled from the kitchen.

"Hurry up. Grab one plate."

Hal and I met up at the kitchen counter. It was the perfect moment to tell him about the essay that I was working on. "It's mainly about Pidgin English," I said, "but I want to write about you too."

"No wayz," he said.

"OK den. Wat?"

"Remember when you were little? You were a late-talker."

"I was?"

"Remember? The other kids used to tease you 'short-tongue.'"

From a sociolinguistic perspective, Elizabeth Carr and Bernhard Hormann recognized the cultural value of Hawaiʻi Creole English. In the 1960 issue of Social Process in Hawaii, Carr and Hormann addressed the social and linguistic complexities involved with the use of Hawaiʻi Creole English without imposing stereotypical labels of ignorance and inadequacy. Carr and Hormann expressed an urgency to change teaching methods so educators would be sensitive to the cultural value of Pidgin while promoting the need to learn Standard English.

The limited view, which for so long prevailed in American education towards foreign languages and "substandard" English speech of immigrant groups and lower-class people, is being superseded by new approaches.

(Hormann **7)**

My little bradda no belong on dat bus wit all dose handicap freaks.

"I kinda remember da short tongue thing," Hal said.

"What do you remember about the Easter Seals school?"

"Not much. I guess I remember being around other handicapped kids."

"Other handicapped kids?" I asked him. He seemed stunned by what he had said.

"Eh, I know I wasn't handicapped; not like them."

"Do you remember how you were treated?"

"Nah. Not really" he told me, then he hesitated for a minute.

"Ya, I guess sometimes... you know, people would talk real loud and slow like I stupid or someting. I got plenny attention but." Hal grinned.

Mom asked Hal to go down to the basement and bring up another case of soda, so while he was downstairs, I asked Mom about Hal. She said she had taken him to his pediatrician, who then referred her to a speech pathologist. "He wouldn't talk," she told me. "We worried. Why you like know?"

I told her about the premise of my essay, how children who spoke exclusively Pidgin were treated like they were handicapped, retarded even, and how they were discriminated against by adul

"But your brother wasn't treated the way those children were treated," my mother said.

"Ma, das my point."

Hal had a real speech disorder. The plantation children did not, and yet, they were treated far worse than he. Hal's speech therapist simply wanted to get Hal to talk. English School System tried to silence local children. In many instances, they did.

"Do you remember how only you could understand what Harold-Boy was saying?" my mother said to me. "We used to call you fo come translate for us."

I remember.

"You know, once Harold-Boy started working wit da speech therapist, he started talking," "After dat, he was very shy. Shame for say anyting. He still li'dat. Drives me nuts." I looked around the living room. Lisa, my future sister-in-law, is only four months pregnant, and Hal has already invested in a new crib, a rocking chair, and a little oak dresser. He and Lisa will get married after the baby is born, after they settle in their little apartment, after some of the hospital bills have been paid. My brother, the kid whose mother was always frustrated by his emotional distance and inability to communicate, was not going to run away and hide.

He comes back into the room carrying a case of soda. "So how do you feel about being a daddy?" I asked him. "Scared," he said, "but happy."

politics and racism.

Try let him sing.

Pidgin and its speakers have an impressive story to tell.

The first generation of immigrant plantation laborers used Hawai'i Pidgin English to foster solidarity amoung themselves even when HPE was used to oppress them. One generation later, corporate leaders and politicians tried to dodge the power of Hawai'i Pidgin English by establishing a linguistic hierarchy that divided the middle-class elite and the working class. Today, we speak Hawai'i Creole English, and despite continued criticism of Pidgin by institutionalized elitism,

Pidgin continues to thrive.

Perhaps Pidgin's perseverance stems from the necessity for resistance. Andrew Lind, who served as editorial adviser to the 1960 issue of Social Process in Hawaii, explains how local speakers of Hawai'i Creole English use Pidgin as a means of resistance towards those who try to suppress it.

Indeed the resistance to the Creole dialect by professional educators and the economic elite frequently strengthens **a stubborn determination to use it...**

If the upper classes disapprove of Island 'pidgin,' one can derive a certain sense of superiority by flaunting before them a tongue in which they are obviously at a disadvantage.

Wot you looking at?
"Badda you?"

Resistance is an intrinsic element of Pidgin.

Today, there are Pidgin speakers who perpetuate the language and its message of resistance through literature. Hawai'i poets, novelists, and playwrights such as Darrell H.Y. Lum, Eric Chock, Lee Tonouchi, Rodney Morales, R. Zamora Linmark, Kathy Kaleokealoha Kaloloahilani Banggo, Juliet S. Kono, Hina Kahanu, Joe Balaz, Alani Apio, Yokanaan Kearns, Kimo Armitage, Gary Pak, Lois-Ann Yamanaka, to name a few, have written literature that both criticizes and heals the inferiority complexes and self-loathing that was created by cultural elitists. This literature, which has received international attention, enlightens speakers of any language, whether indigenous, Creole, or dominant, about the politics of language.

It is useless to do a value comparison between any language. Any type of language should never function as a barrier between peoples, let alone serve to oppress or repress. As sociologist Bernhard L. Hormaan wrote in his article "Hawaii's Liguistic Situation: A Sociological Interpretation in the New Key," to impose the use of one standard language is

"itself a kind of provincialism for it implies an inability and unwillingness to transcend one's existing horizons".

(31)

It is necessary to consider the positive social value of all types of language. Speakers of Creole languages should never be perceived as mere casualties of insularity, ignorance, and social isolation. The history of Hawai'i Creole English has inspiring accounts of resourcefulness, intellect, and competence that both reflect and sustain local Hawai'i culture.

Ngugi Wa Thiong'o, author of Decolonising the Mind, explains how language, culture, and self-image are interdependent upon each other.

{ **... language as culture is an image-forming agent in the mind of a child.** Our conception of ourselves as a people, individually and collectively, is based on those pictures and images which may or may not correctly correspond to the actual reality of the struggles with **nature and nurture** which produced them in the first place. But our capacity to confront the world creatively is dependent on how those images correspond or not to the reality, how they distort or clarify the reality of our struggles... Thus a specific culture is not transmitted through language in its universality but in its particularity as the language of a specific community with a specific history.

When local Hawaiʻi students hear the rhythms of their own voices in their own literature, they are pleasantly shocked. It is as if they had never imagined their world was significant enough to be in the pages of a book.

Afta dat, dey talk up. Dey not so scared fo speak up anymo.

Hawaiʻi Creole English: History and Social Attitudes

Carr, Elizabeth Ball. Da Kine Talk: From Pidgin to Standard English in Hawaiʻi. Honolulu:Hawaiʻi, 1972.

Hormann, Bernhard L. "Hawaii's Linguistic Situation: A Sociological Interpretation in the New Key." Social Process in Hawaii. Honolulu: University of Hawaiʻi, 1960.

Hughes, Judith R. "The Demise of the English Standard School System in Hawaiʻi." The Hawaiian Journal of History. 27 (1993): 65-89.

Kawamoto, Kevin Y. "Hegemony and Language Politics in Hawaiʻi." World Englishes. 12 (1993): 193-207.

Lind, Andrew. "Communication: A Problem of Island Youth." Social Process in Hawaii. 24 (1960):44-53.

Ngugi Wa Thiong'o. Decolonizing the Mind: The Politics of Language in African Literature. London: J. Currey; Portsmouth, N.H.: Heinemann, 1986.

Reinecke, John E., "The Competition of Languages in Hawaiʻi." Social Process in Hawaii. 2 (1936): 7-10.

---. Language and Dialect in Hawaii; A Sociolinguistic History to 1935. Revision of the author's thesis, University of Hawaiʻi, 1935. Honolulu: University of Hawaiʻi, 1969.

Romaine, Suzanne. "Hawaiʻi Creole English as a Literary Language." Language in Society. 23 (1994): 527:554.

Sato, Charlene. "Language Attitudes and Sociolinguistic Variation in Hawaiʻi." University of Hawaiʻi Working Papers in ESL. 8 (1989): 191-216.

Smith, Madorah. "A Study of The Causes of Feelings of Inferiority." Reprinted from The Journal of Psychology, 5 (1938): 315-332.

---. Some Light on the Problem of Bilingualism As Found From a Study of The

Progress in Mastery of English Among Preschool Children of Non-American Ancestry in Hawai'i. Provincetown: The Journal Press, 1939.

Territory of Hawai'i. Department of Public Instruction, Division of Elementary Education. Hawai'i Speech Needs Analysis and Improvement of Island Speech. Hawai'i: DPI, 1949.

Tsai, Michael. "Pondering Pidgin." Honolulu Weekly. 3 (1995).

Yamamoto, J. "The Perception and Stereotyping of Speech Varieties in Hawai'i." University of Hawai'i Working Papers in Linguistics. 14 (1982): 75-88.

Speech Disorders

Hanson, Marvin L. Articulation. Philadelphia: W.B. Saunders, 1983.

Johnson, Wendell. ed. Speech Handicapped School Children. Iowa: University of Iowa, 1975.

Kersner, Myra and Jannet A. Wright. ed. How to Manage Communication Problems in Young Children. 2nd ed. London: David Fulton, 1996.

Renfrew, C.E. Speech Disorders in Children. Oxford: Pergamon, 1972.

Rousey, Carol E. A Practical Guide to Helping Children with Speech and Language Problems: For Parents and Teachers Only. Springfield: C.C. Thomas, 1984.